Nenshu
and the Tiger

Martin Bell

Nenshu and the Tiger

Parables of Life and Death

THE SEABURY PRESS · NEW YORK

1981
The Seabury Press
815 Second Avenue
New York, N.Y. 10017

Copyright © 1975 by Martin Bell
Designed by Carol Basen
Music autography by Maxwell Weaner
Printed in the United States of America

All New Testament quotations are from the Revised Standard Version, Copyright 1946 by Division of Christian Education of the National Council of the Churches of Christ in the United States of America.

LIBRARY OF CONGRESS CATALOGING IN PUBLICATION DATA

Bell, Martin.
  Nenshu and the tiger.

  SUMMARY: Stories, songs, and poems reflecting Christian values.
  [1. Christian life—Fiction. 2. Short stories]
I. Title.
PZ 7.B41154Ne [Fic] 74-32042
ISBN 0-8164-2356-3

Contents

Nenshu
and the Tiger

Nenshu
and the Tiger

I

NATURALLY, it could have been described in another way. Nenshu wondered if his own confusion had prompted him to present a distorted version of the facts. Perhaps he had misinterpreted the event, omitted a significant detail, unnecessarily added some dimension of horror.

Nenshu was quite unable to cope with human suffering. So out of his own anxiety and rage had he misrepresented historical occurrence?

It was possible.

But the wolf. Surely the wolf could penetrate to the core of what had happened. Nenshu did not believe that the wolf would allow himself to be misled by the unreliable report of a fallible messenger.

Mysterious, implacable, and ever so dangerous, the great silver wolf had walked coincidentally with chronological order since the dawn of creation. Everything that was, he had decreed to be necessary. Even atrocity and death were vehicles of his unearthly purpose. Nenshu did not know why, and he had never dared to ask.

Curious then that the frightened messenger felt

partly responsible for bringing about the end of time.

II

The boy had been crucified. Nenshu told the story as briefly as possible. And then he waited.

For a moment it looked as if the wolf had stopped breathing. He did not move or speak. Yet, in the next instant, something remarkable happened. The animal closed his eyes.

Nenshu could not remember ever seeing the wolf close his eyes before. It made him uneasy. To behold so awful and robust a creature with his eyes tightly closed is more difficult than one might imagine.

Nenshu was surprised by the wolf's response. Why had this death been so special?

"Why so special, Nenshu?" the wolf said reading his thoughts. "Perhaps because I am lonely and the boy loved me more than life itself. Perhaps because I am old and tired and sick of man's inhumanity to God. Perhaps because this time they have gone too far."

The wolf spoke more deliberately now. "Why so special, Nenshu? Perhaps only because I say so."

III

Nenshu sensed that something had changed. He stared at the wolf. And what he saw was definitely not to his liking. It was uncanny.

The wolf looked the same as he had the moment before—only backwards. Evidently he had turned himself inside-out, doubled back upon himself, and then returned.

The energy thus created was almost unbearable. Nenshu felt very cold.

Somewhere in what human beings call time and space many beheld a temple curtain that had been torn in half on the day preceding.

As yet they did not understand anything.

"This people's heart has grown dull," said the wolf. "And their ears are heavy of hearing, and their eyes they have closed, lest they should perceive with their eyes, and hear with their ears, and understand with their heart, and turn for me to heal them."

Nenshu lost all sense of balance, proportion, and depth. The backwards-wolf began to howl in a terrifying manner. Then two worlds came into collision.

Suddenly, the bewildered messenger was precipitated into chronology. Yet by some miracle he remained in the eternal realm as well. Nenshu realized with fascination that he was indeed both somewhere and nowhere at the same time.

But what time was that?

Surrounded by worldly darkness, Nenshu found

himself utterly alone and with no idea of what to do next. So he made the best decision possible.

He waited.

"It will be daylight soon," he thought. "When the sun comes up, I will be able to see where I am."

After a few minutes Nenshu was aware that the place had a peculiar fragrance. Herbs and spices, most certainly.

"Perhaps I am in a garden, then?"

Nenshu stood patiently, his eyes straining for the first glimpse of dawn.

IV

The half-light just before dawn revealed a small garden and some men sleeping near a tomb which had been cut out of the rock. Nenshu noticed that a large stone covered the tomb's entrance. "How curious," he thought. "I am in a garden."

Quietly, Nenshu waited for the sun to appear. He attributed his sense of expectancy and joy to the kind of breathless anticipation one experiences just before any sunrise. After all, he had no reason to look for anything else.

Nenshu's gaze was fixed on the sky. Without realizing it, of course, he was looking in the wrong place.

From the partial darkness of Joseph's garden a boy's voice whispered, "Nenshu!"

The startled messenger turned toward the

tomb. At first he did not believe what his eyes told him was there. Somehow, without a sound, the large stone had been rolled away. And standing silently in the tomb's entrance was the boy who had been crucified.

"Good morning, Nenshu," he said softly. Then smiling, he added, "Please be careful not to awaken these good men who are sleeping. They have been up most of the night."

Nenshu stared at the boy. He didn't look right. Something was amiss or out of place. Almost immediately, however, he realized what had happened, and he shuddered. Nothing was wrong. Everything was in order.

The boy was the same—only backwards.

Barely audible, Nenshu said, "The very stone which the builders rejected has become the head of the corner; this was the wolf's doing and it is marvelous to behold."

The boy motioned for Nenshu to follow. Hurriedly, they left the garden.

The sun was visible now. Two women made their way along a path that led toward the empty sepulcher.

"How will they ever understand?" thought Nenshu as he began to run in order to keep up with the reverse-figure that went before him.

V

Not until they reached a place called Galilee did the boy stop for rest. When Nenshu reflected upon the trip he realized that they had done the impossible. Both of them had been on the road for days.

Now the boy sat easily on a rock by the side of the path. "Wolf eyes," thought the messenger. "He has wolf eyes."

Nenshu spoke boldly. "Sir, are you a wolf in boy's clothing, or a boy in wolf's clothing?"

"What a perfect question," said the backwards one. "In truth, I am neither. Or both, perhaps. Well, neither, really. What I mean is: I am a boy; I am a wolf."

"Sir," Nenshu went on, "are we in time or out of it now? I must confess that I am thoroughly lost."

There on the rock facing Nenshu sat the great, silver wolf. "Both in time and out of it," the animal said gently. "This is high-time. Worlds in collision. Chronology has ended. Yet, naturally, it must, and will, continue until the last day. They just went too far, Nenshu. Much too far. Nothing can ever be the same again."

"But you, sir," the messenger ventured cautiously. "You are the same, are you not?"

The wolf looked tired. "Yes, that is true. I am the same. Nothing at all can change me. Nevertheless, I shall continue to create and redeem at will. What you are experiencing presently is a wholly New Creation. High-time. Worlds in collision."

Now the boy sat where the wolf had been. "I have a question for you, Nenshu," he said. "How will human beings explain what has transpired here? And who will they say that I am?"

Nenshu replied carefully. "They will not understand. However, I believe that the New Creation, high-time, will be a cause for rejoicing among them. Still, in order to answer more intelligently, I must ask one further question. Will they see you?"

"Yes," answered the boy. "They will see me."

"Then there will be a multiplicity of response, sir. Some will say that you are a wolf in boy's clothing. Others the opposite. Many will disbelieve all that they see. It will cause quite an uproar, you know. Much disagreement. To-the-death commitments. Persecutions, even wars. All manner of things will be manifest in this New Creation. It will not be safe for anyone."

"Precisely," said the wolf.

"All part of your unearthly purpose, no doubt," said Nenshu. "However, this is most definitely going to disrupt history, sir. Yes, indeed. Highly disruptive, this New Creation."

The wolf was silent.

Nenshu had nothing further to say. He just wondered what was going to happen next. Thus, neither of them spoke for several hours.

Then, suddenly, the boy said, "But what about Nenshu? Who does he say that I am?"

Nenshu smiled. "That is an easy question, sir. You are the Tiger, of course."

"Precisely," said the wolf. And then together they waited for the first disciples to arrive.

Visitation

"EACH of us is only running toward his death," she continued. "But then no one seems to be able to stop the running. Did you realize that St. Gregory considered sorrow to be a capital sin?"

"No," I commented without moving. "I didn't know that. Really."

She placed her fingers flat on the table edge. For one who is a small-talk detester, I thought, I'm doing quite well. I had been listening with what must have seemed like ferocious concentration for over fifteen minutes. Actually, there was nothing to lose.

I am intrigued by the restless—the discontents of our society, you might say. And besides, I could feel her smiling in my direction. The satisfied, the satiated might tactfully refuse such a dislocating experience. Not me. I am like an old hinge swinging in the wind. I need attention.

"You actually are quite free," she said, now lying on her back on the floor, "since the paradox of man resolves itself in unconditional silence for the most part."

"I don't get it," was my carefully thought-out reply.

"Of course not," she laughed, suddenly inspired. "The whole thing is already infinitely complex, and there is every chance that it will lead somewhere even more mysterious before we're through."

Now she sat up and began talking to herself in earnest. "I have lived this way for longer than you might imagine. My imprecision and lack of uniformity are real enough. Just as your pretending to be disagreeable is not."

"Soon, you will fall in love with me," I ventured.

"Oh, without a doubt," she smiled. "In fact, I already have. Amidst all the jostling, shoving, and devouring of one another, we must find love."

I felt there was a point that needed to be made. She was so obscurely wild and unstable. I could no longer remain anonymous.

"And I will love you, too." The words created a ratcheting sound.

"Yes, that's so," she replied. "You will love me and ours will be an indestructable unity."

She said that and then just walked away, leaving me like a clown in the center ring, swimming in dust and magnesium rays, mumbling that the show must go on.

BURNING FOUNTAIN

I don't guess the hard part will be leav-ing all the dreams be-hind. That would hap-pen an-y-way; they van-ish like the wind. It's lone-li-ness of this sort that makes free-dom just a state of mind. I'll have to ask you in a way that will be-tray my soul. Did you find ____ the burn-ing foun-tain ____ or your king - dom by the sea? ____ And if I ____ should reach the moun-tain ____ would you still ____ make room for me?

BURNING FOUNTAIN

1. I don't guess the hard part
     will be leaving all the dreams behind.
   That would happen anyway;
     they vanish like the wind.
   It's loneliness of this sort
     that makes freedom just a state of mind.
   I'll have to ask you in a way
     that will betray my soul.

> *Did you find the burning fountain*
> *Or your kingdom by the sea?*
> *And if I should reach the mountain*
> *Would you still make room for me?*

2. I'll be damned if it didn't happen
     just the way they said it would;
   And I learned a new respect for those
     who've gone before our time.
   It's a longer and a harder way
     than I had ever counted on.
   And the more I follow freedom
     the more I learn to die.

*Did you find the burning fountain
Or your kingdom by the sea?
And if I should reach the mountain
Would you still make room for me?*

costs plenty

been writing more or less complicated lyrics to
franklin roosevelt type songs for somewhere
over one quarter century she

got tired of telling it like it was but couldn't
quite bring herself to tell it like it wasn't which
is all probably to her credit although it sure
didn't leave her holding many of the cards

took the elevated train to fifty third street daily
and never dreamed she'd get derailed before
her fifty second birthday but then you never
can tell

used to buy legal pads instead of groceries and
then reach in the cupboard whenever she
wanted to get annoyed

found out it costs plenty to pay attention and
when you don't give a damn the price goes up
illusion is cheap though just not very singable
besides it looks funny on the printed page

one good thing anyway she learned discipline
doesn't always come in cans and a songwriter
ought to know stuff like that since there are lots
of cant's involved and life gets awfully real
when you know the score

in short she took many long walks to get her
circulation going even though hardly anyone
seemed to be picking up on fdr lyrics and she
kept running into lots of no thanks advice and
out of legal pads

night time was the hardest beat to write for
since there were no set counts to the bars and
all that syncopated sleeping without rests
brought her down to a place where fifty second
hadn't even come up and she was derailed

a shattering experience true but not all bad by a
long shot it left her scared and scarred but
otherwise intact and thereafter she kept a box
of pencils in the refrigerator to remind herself
that you can't eat more or less complicated
lyrics to franklin roosevelt type songs

got a job as a waitress when she was fifty two
and resolved not to spend any more money on
legal pads nights were even more difficult to
chart therefore and naturally life didn't stop
being real

thought once or twice about buying a teddy
bear and probably should have done just that
but instead her old compulsion grabbed hold
one night and wouldn't turn loose all the stores
were closed so she started writing a new song
on some old paper towels god what a struggle
words didn't fit rhymes wouldn't do spent the
whole night in the bathroom too only light she
had except for the refrigerator by morning she
needed to blow her nose and there weren't any
paper towels left

spread out in front of her on the bathroom floor
lay a whole night's work damn peculiar song she
thought bewildered by her own handwriting it
said

help me

well it's true her songs didn't ever sell very
good but that was one great lady on the
bathroom floor i hope to shout and it hurts a lot
to tell about her

makes me want to love you enough not to
protect you at all

Life Is Like
A Card Game

I LIKE to work picture puzzles. In fact, it's one of my favorite pastimes. I have endless amounts of patience for such activity. Never seem to get frustrated.

No matter how long it takes, the puzzle will finally go together. All the pieces will fit because they were designed to fit. They have to fit. It's impossible to cram two mismatched pieces together and be satisfied with the result.

Picture puzzles are conclusional. They may take a long time to complete, but patience and persistence will be rewarded.

Not so with card games. Especially gin rummy. Here I am constantly having to make decisions about the future of my hand based on a paucity of data.

For instance, should I keep the jack of clubs or should I throw it away? I don't know what's going to happen. I don't know what's in my partner's hand. And, more difficult, I don't know what's in the pile. Still, it's my turn. And I have to play.

I may make just the right decision and thereby consider myself to be a wise fellow indeed. In such an event I have overlooked the contingent nature of the facts. After all, this is an opportunity for boasting about my cunning and skill.

On the other hand, the decision may bring disaster—even the end of the game. Now I am more likely to curse fate, or my partner, or the cards.

I prefer making picture puzzles. It's relaxing. Sooner or later I know everything is going to fit together. Card games are terribly frustrating. I can get angry playing cards.

Putting together a picture puzzle is a matter of discovery and conclusion. Each puzzle is based upon a pre-designed harmony and order. All that is required of the participant is to work diligently and systematically. There will come a time when everything falls into place.

But card games require one decision after another. And not once is there enough data provided to make an entirely competent play. There is always present the element of risk and the threat of ultimate failure. That's the nature of the game. When it's your turn, you decide on the basis of the facts at your disposal.

To complicate matters further, the cards never demand one specific choice. Many decisions are possible. It isn't a case of either/or. No two persons would play the same series of hands identically. The whole thing is tremendously complex.

Like my father used to say, card games are frustrating, and unnerving—and challenging.

Oh, I almost forgot: it's your deal.

WILL IT ALL BE WORTH IT IN THE END?

Geor - gia. Well, I've nev - er   seen At - lan - ta   in   the   spring.

WILL IT ALL BE WORTH IT IN THE END?

CHORUS: *Will it all be worth it in the end?*
             Will the road we're traveling ever
             bend?
             I'd like an honest answer, friend.
             Will it all be worth it in the end?

1. Here I go again. I hardly know my
   name
   I'm so tired.
   I wonder how it is that every airport
   finally looks the same.
   Monday night I leave Detroit for
   Pittsburgh,
       Then New York and on to
       Georgia.
   Well, I've never seen Atlanta in the
   spring.

       [*chorus*]

2. Here I go again. The plane is climb-
   ing high.
   It seems as if I've lost all my direction

In an unfamiliar sky.
There's nothing that I haven't dared
   to dream of,
   But you have shared the dreams,
      love,
And you know they're mostly heart-
   breaks in disguise.

[*chorus*]

3. Here I go again. I bought myself a
   Bible.
   Well, it's a way to kill some time
      Until I catch the plane from Den-
         ver to L.A.
   And I'm reading in the book of
      Revelation
      About how the warring nations of
         this world
   Will face the wrath of God someday.

[*chorus*]

Arnold

ONCE there was a bird with fur. He had a long yellow beak and pleasant green eyes. Everyone who knew him called him Arnold. But his real name was Bill.

Bill would never fly when he wanted to go somewhere. He was more than satisfied to shuffle along the ground at a leisurely pace. And sooner or later he always got where he was going.

Usually, when a group of his friends saw Bill shuffling quietly to or fro they would say, "Hello, Arnold!" And Bill would say, "Hello." And then after he was gone the whole group would spend a lot of time talking about all of the reasons why Arnold should fly instead of shuffle.

It made Bill happy whenever friends said hello to him. And he rather liked the name "Arnold," even though it wasn't his name. Interestingly enough, Bill didn't know that his friends thought he should fly, because no one ever told him what they said when he wasn't there.

Now and then Bill was mistaken for a kitten. This was in part due to his appearance, of course. But it was also because he could, and did, purr whenever he wanted to.

Perhaps you have never seen a bird with fur that shuffles and purrs. Certainly, the same is true about many others. So please don't be discouraged. But do stay alert. Heads up and all that could avoid many a passing-by-unnoticed.

Anyway, "Arnold," as he was called, enjoyed life immensely. And although he had only one possession, it was enough. I wonder if you can guess what he had? Would it surprise you to learn that Bill owned a wrist watch? Well, he did. On one furry wing Bill wore a tiny Timex brand wrist watch.

The watch didn't work. And so Bill never really knew what time it was. Still, he was always hopeful that someone might notice it there on his wing and ask, "What's the time?" Bill chuckled softly when he thought about his reply. Naturally, he would make up a time. And then without so much as blinking a green eye he would say, "It's 3:45." Or perhaps, "Ten-fifteen by my watch." He could decide on whatever time he wanted. Such fun to own a watch that didn't work.

II

Glenda the bobcat liked "Arnold." Ordinarily birds weren't safe when she was around. Not at all. But, as luck would have it, Glenda was terribly nearsighted. And she actually did think that Bill was a tiny bobcat. (You may be certain he had never indicated otherwise.) Whenever Glenda found Bill shuffling, she always carried him back to her lair by the fur of his neck. Then Bill would purr for a long while until Glenda went looking for food. When the coast was clear, so to speak, he shuffled on about his own business—until she found him again, and the process was repeated.

During the various interludes between being found by Glenda and waiting for someone to ask about the time, Bill spent many a happy hour pretending to wind his watch. I say "pretending" because it is nearly impossible to wind anything with a wing. It wasn't that Bill didn't try. He just never succeeded.

III

Finally the day came when one of his friends approached him on behalf of the entire group who had been insisting that he should fly.

"Arnold," he asked cautiously, "why don't you ever fly?" It was Charles, the groundhog.

"Because flying is for the birds, Charles," replied Bill, shuffling around a bit as if to emphasize the point.

"But you *are* a bird, Arnold," the groundhog insisted. "And you really ought to fly. You're making everybody uncomfortable."

Bill was silent. He looked perplexed and lost in thought. Then, after a moment or two, he brightened up and said, "No, I don't think so, Charles. I

don't want to fly. I'm sorry it makes you uncomfortable. Truly I am. However, flying is out of the
question."

"But, Arnold," said the exasperated groundhog,
"what shall I tell the others? You're embarrassing
all of us."

"Tell them anything you want to, Charles. Just
get the point across. No flying. I'm sorry." Bill
glanced at his watch. "Why, however did it get to
be so late? It's 8:37—past your suppertime,
Charles. Time for me to be on my way, too." Bill
seemed genuinely surprised and chagrined by the
lateness of the hour. "Thank you for stopping,
though. I know it took a great deal of courage to
be spokesman for the entire group. Goodnight,
Charles. Can you believe the time? Wherever did
the evening go?"

After the confused groundhog had scurried off
in order to make it home for supper, Bill sat down
in the warm afternoon sun. He decided to make up
a shuffling song to sing while moving about.

> Shuffle, shuffle to and fro
> I'll get where I'm going.
> Never even have to know
> Which way the wind is blowing.

> I suppose that I could fly,
> There's really nothing to it.
> Still, I've always wondered why
> A bird would want to do it.

There, that was a fine song. Bill smiled as he thought about Charles running home for supper. Then he placed both wings behind his neck and lay back in the grass for a short nap.

> Shuffle, shuffle to and fro
> I'll get where I'm going.
> Never even have to know
> Which way . . . the . . . wind . . .

Soon, Bill was asleep. The afternoon sun warmed his fur and he dreamed an appropriate dream.

IV

After a while he heard a voice beside him saying, "Hello, Arnold." Slowly, Bill opened one eye. It was nearly dark. Evidently, he'd slept a good bit longer than he planned. "Hello, Arnold." Bill turned in the direction of the greeting. It was a firefly acquaintance.

"Hello, Alice. Nice evening and all," he said pleasantly.

"Arnold, will you tell me what's going on? Whatever did you say to upset Charles so? Why won't you fly like you're supposed to? And what are you doing lying here in the grass?" Alice seemed puzzled and concerned.

"Why, of course, I'll tell you, Alice," said Bill,

dusting himself off and resuming an upright position. His green eyes reflected the firefly's glittering. He blinked at Alice once or twice and then began.

"For the most part, I'm convinced that we forest animals—birds, groundhogs, even fireflies—take ourselves too seriously. Each of us seems to believe that he or she has a certain set part to act out in some great big cosmic play. Incidentally, I don't think that's true, Alice. But, God knows, it might be. All I'm saying is that either way, it's funny. If there really is a script, the whole idea tickles me. And if there isn't any script at all, but we keep insisting on acting out a part that hasn't even been assigned to us, then that's hilarious."

Alice looked distressed. "I don't think it's funny, Arnold. Everyone knows there is a script. And it's very important that you act the way you are supposed to. Your part *has* been assigned."

Bill shuffled some. "Perhaps," he said.

Alice waited for a minute or two and then she added, "Arnold, are you OK?"

"Oh, yes. Fine, fine. I was just thinking that I am more of a mind to believe the play isn't composed until after the actors themselves have created the script by what they say and do. I'm sure we take ourselves much too seriously, Alice." Bill pretended to wind his watch.

"Is that a wrist watch, Arnold?"

"Why, yes it is," Bill replied without looking up. "Yes, indeed. It is—a wrist watch. And a favorite possession of mine, too."

"What's the time?" Alice asked.

Without so much as blinking a green eye, Bill said, "It's nearly midnight. Eleven fifty-four to be exact."

"Gracious, Arnold! Are you sure? It doesn't seem that late."

"Am I sure? Oh, yes, certainly—11:54 exactly. It's always later than we think, you know." Bill looked up and blinked thoughtfully.

"Goodnight, Arnold," mumbled the bewildered firefly.

"Goodnight, Alice. And thanks for stopping."

V

That night Bill slept out under the stars. He awoke feeling refreshed and even more delighted with his world than ever. For a while he pretended to wind his watch.

Shuffle, shuffle. To and fro. A bird with fur. A long yellow beak and pleasant green eyes. "I'm sure we take ourselves much too seriously," he mumbled while making an attempt to stand on his head. Then, upside-down, Bill saw Glenda the bobcat headed earnestly in his direction, and he immediately toppled over in silent laughter. "There can be no mistake about it," he thought. "We do take ourselves much too seriously."

ARNOLD'S SONG

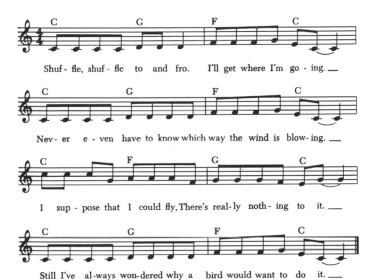

Shuf - fle, shuf - fle to and fro. I'll get where I'm go - ing. ___

Nev - er e - ven have to know which way the wind is blow - ing. ___

I sup - pose that I could fly, There's real - ly noth - ing to it. ___

Still I've al - ways won - dered why a bird would want to do it. ___

Words and music copyright © 1975 by Martin Bell

I Tend
to Shout More

Today I carry less of
                what we used to
Call composure.
I'm less serene.
Less well
         thought out. I
     tend to shout
            more.
I'm growing older.

A younger man would
         know
       full well that
         all
Of this must
     change
If given time.
But time is
     never given. Only
       taken,
Or rearranged.

Unimaginable,
   the weariness
  that forty
Years has
   earned.
I am elect.
The chosen one—by hazard,
     really.
I have
  been burned.

And yet
   for now we're
   standing very close.
The
  night surrounds.
By dark released,
You
  touch
   me and the tension
  dissipates.
Your grace abounds.

I never wait
  for
   offered
  certainty. I
  simply live it.
Inward journey.
City
  drab
  and dead.

Amidst a chaos of
                    complexity,
        I
May survive yet.

Survive, perhaps,
                is much
        too harsh
        a word. The call
                        is
For running free.
Angelic hosts
Proclaim
            the folly of survival.
    And with
            one voice they
    Overturn
                analogies that
Frighten and exploit
            the Spirit.

            (Conceive of it not
                bodily, for
            It is meant
                ghostly.)

Why is it that we
            keep the most
                important things
            unspoken?
Hanging in air.

As you are
       leaving now,
I could just
          stare. Remembering
     how you
Have
    been
      broken.

Dark silhouette
    glittering
    on the
        current of
         our
        interchange.
To hell with that!

It's
    words
      you need.
A someone
     who
     will come flat out
     and say it.
Well, I'm your man.

Duck Drank Too Much

Duck drank too much
More fun than a whole big
      bag of jelly beans
Wow

Mrs. Duck said once
And it she said a thousand
      times for sure
Stop

Kept going anyway
Didn't give one good quack
      Mrs. Duck what she said
No

Got drunk lots Duck
Sang loud songs real tears cried
      found some truth too
Good

Eccentric Duck
Loads rather drink gin than
      swim in the mill pond
Weird

Already gave cat
Today some tender vittles in
    a bowl Mrs. Duck
Meow

Sure kind to cat
But tonight when Duck got back
    bleah bleah bleah
Yeah

Drank whole bottle wine
Went out for swim quick
    in the mill pond
Splash

Paddled tiny bit around
Climbed out soon shook feathers dry
    felt good and high
Nice

Happy Duck quack quack
Crooked waddled down path got home
    supper much too late
Whoops

Cheerie Duck most part
Mrs. Duck yelled nuts he was
    should be in bin
Looney

All wrong said Duck

Smiled and fixed supper his own
      then watched TV
Color

Got ready for bed
Set out saucer gin for cat
      had good night's sleep
Z-Z-Z-Z

Woke up refreshed
Drank two beers then yes crooked
      waddled off to work
Factory

Pleasant Duck all day
Mrs. Duck got gray and nearly
      ended up in hatch
Booby

Pastor Duck stepped in
Going to end up one in hatch
      other in bin
Quit

So Duck he stopped
Mrs. Duck felt better much and cat
      drank milk again
Yuk

Happy ending story this

Two sober ducks one sober cat
    all three really glad
Not bad

BYPASSED BY THE HIGHWAY

1. In six - ty four they tore the sta - tion
2. Now they've run a high - way through the

down. Lord, _____ the times are chang - ing. ___
town, but I _____ can still re - mem - ber ___

There be - hind the drug - store's where the box - cars used to be.
Ear - ly ev - ery morn - ing when the steel rail caught the sun.

That's what I keep see - ing. _____
I don't care for high - ways. ___

Chorus

Grand - pa used to drive a truck and I would ride be - hind.

We would take the mail down to the train.

I could drink my cof - fee black when I was on - ly nine, and I

tried as hard as an - y oth - er man.

Tried as hard as an - y oth - er man.

3. One day Grand - pa had to say good - bye. Well, I
4. six - ty four they tore the sta - tion down. The ___

guessed ___ that he'd be leav - ing. ___
town ___ keeps right on chang - ing. ___ It

Then my own re - flec - tion in the win - dows of the train
took me quite a while but now I fin - ally un - der - stand;

seemed ___ a lit - tle old - er. ___ In

I was by - passed by the high - way. ___

Chorus
Grand - pa used to drive a truck and I would ride be - hind.

We would take the mail down to the train.

I could drink my cof - fee black when I was on - ly nine,   and I

tried   as   hard   as   an - y   oth - er   man.

Tried as hard as an - y oth - er man.   Now I think I fin- ally un- der-

stand.   Tried as hard as   an - y   oth - er   man.

BYPASSED BY THE HIGHWAY

1. In sixty-four they tore the station down.
   Lord, the times are changing.
   There behind the drugstore's where
      the boxcars used to be.
   That's what I keep seeing.

2. Now they've run a highway through the town,
   But I can still remember
   Early every morning when the steel rail
      caught the sun.
   I don't care for highways.

   > *Grandpa used to drive a truck*
   > *and I would ride behind.*
   > *We would take the mail down to the*
   >   *train.*
   > *I could drink my coffee black*
   >   *when I was only nine,*
   > *And I tried as hard as any other man.*

3. One day Grandpa had to say goodbye.
   Well, I guessed that he'd be leaving.
   Then my own reflection in the windows
      of the train
   Seemed a little older.

4. In sixty-four they tore the station down.
   The town keeps right on changing.
   It took me quite a while but now
      I finally understand;
   I was bypassed by the highway.

> *Grandpa used to drive a truck*
>   *and I would ride behind.*
> *We would take the mail down to the*
>   *train.*
> *I could drink my coffee black*
>   *when I was only nine,*
> *And I tried as hard as any other man.*

Crazy Mary Katherine

EVERYBODY gets really angry when I tell them I'll be happy to give the money, only I don't want to count my blessings. One lady says thanksgiving is the only real motivation for any giving, and it's unamerican not to be thankful. She's serious. Mary Katherine, she says, you're unamerican.

That's wrong, you know. I'm not unamerican. And I am thankful. I just don't want to go around counting my blessings. There's a difference between being thankful and counting your blessings. I learned that in church. And if I hadn't learned it in church, it's for sure I would have learned it in the hospital.

"Giving is dying," I say rather too loudly, without fully realizing that I have spoken. My visitors are somewhat taken aback. "It should be abundantly clear that giving does ever so much for the giver," they continue almost in unison. "If your gift is motivated properly, the act of giving will make you *feel* good." "No, not at all," I insist, "That's poppycock. Any giving whatsoever—whether it is an unexpected loss, a contribution, or a sacrifice, is a form of death."

Now I've gone too far. Everyone just stares at me. I try to look as cheerful as possible, but nobody seems to appreciate what I have said. "Mary Katherine," they say, "you're ungrateful. You have your health, a lovely home in Thunderbird Heights, three wonderful children, and a husband who loves you. God has been good to you." One lady leans forward in her chair and looks at me intently to see what impression these words have made. I am tempted to say thank God that I am not as other women, but the irony of it would be wasted. "I'm getting depressed," I say quietly. "All of this is making me very depressed."

What I don't understand is how they ever got the idea of counting your blessings in the first place. But then, it's entirely possible that I'm not thinking very clearly. My doctor tells me that I don't always think the same way other people do. That's why I ended up in the hospital. Some hospital. The woman across the hall tried to hang herself, a sixteen-year-old cut both her wrists with a razor blade, and I got stuck with this crazy roommate who kept on rocking a *rag doll*, for god's sake, and pretending it was her little girl who had died. They sent me there to get well, but I don't think I made it. What did happen was that I grew up in a hurry. And right in the middle of it all, I learned a whole lot about what it means to be thankful.

Being thankful means saying yes to life in spite of all the obvious suffering and brokenness and guilt that's involved. It means enduring unbearable hardships for no other reason than to show up again tomorrow and be part of this whole wild cosmic adventure. Being thankful means recognizing that all of life is good—not enjoyable or easy, certainly—but necessary and received. To give thanks is to have the courage to get up in the morning. And that doesn't have anything at all to do with counting your blessings.

The room is awfully quiet. I ask if anyone would like tea. Evidently not. Perhaps a glass of sherry? Nothing, then? I ask one perfectly nice woman why she wants to build a wall of separation between me and my former hospital roommate. She says she wants no such thing. I say she does. Everyone thinks I am acting very crazy.

I decide to say what is on my mind. "If I thank God for my three lovely children," I begin, "it's just like saying how glad I am that I don't have a rag doll. And even though I'm very glad about my children and everything, I don't want to thank God for them by way of comparing myself with people whose children are dead. Rather, it is necessary to thank God for all things—for life and for death—for children and for rag dolls. Anything else is a profound expression of sin because it is arrogance, and it separates me from my hospital roommate. The whole idea of counting my blessings makes me sick."

My visitors all look a little frightened now. I don't think they understand about the rag doll or about my roommate or anything. The way it looks to me, I either have to stop talking or risk losing all contact with the ladies in my living room. I decide to stop talking. But it's too late. The words keep right on coming.

"I want to give you money," I say, rising up out of my chair. "Only you must never suggest that giving makes a person *feel* good or anything like that. It isn't fair to misrepresent the facts. Giving is dying, pure and simple. It means renouncing the illusion that life is about security. I used to believe in security, you know. But no more. It is in dying that we live."

"My roommate got out of the hospital two months before I did. One day she walked over to the window and just stood there looking out. I remember she was holding her make-believe child very tight and sort of moaning. The next minute she turned around and held out the rag doll. 'Here,' she said, 'I want you to have this. I don't need it any more.' I was real scared. I didn't know whether to take her doll or not. Then all of a sudden I realized that she wanted to live. My roommate was giving up the only security that she had in all the world because she wanted to live. I took the doll from her and we both wept. For three hours I sat and hugged that doll. I probably should have hugged my roommate, but I never thought of that. The following Tuesday her doctor said that she could go home."

"In a way I suppose I'm glad that I had to go to the hospital. A lot of things got cleared up for me there. But that doesn't mean it made me feel good. I had to give up a lot of illusions about myself and about my world. And any kind of giving, whether it is an unexpected loss, a contribution, or a sacrifice, is a form of death. I find it necessary to believe that it is in dying that we live. But I don't find it possible to believe that in dying we feel good."

My guests are saying goodbye. They are looking at me very strangely, and I can't really blame them. I am a bit unusual. But everything I have said is true, and if they are going to ask people to give freely and sacrificially, then they definitely ought to tell the truth themselves. Evidently they have forgotten about the money. I must be sure to mail them a check.

"They're probably still talking about crazy Mary Katherine," I say out loud. For some reason the thought makes me laugh. I'm not nearly so depressed as I was.

Apostrophe

Yet another interlude.
       A major theme, perhaps?
An organizing principle
      by which
    my thoughts
    are structured
And withheld from
         passion's
     genuine
     excess.
A steaming cup of coffee—
    Now erase.
A poet is
       his life. The life his
    poem.
Romantic fictionizing, yes.
But somewhere
    there
    beneath the charming
       systematic
       word bouquet,
Uncompromising truth.

A bedrock
                    of perplexity.
The sudden
         up-against it
         of
                    my finitude.

The Prodigal .

I WAS angry and would not go in: therefore came my father out. I wonder why my father did that? So many things remain a mystery—not comprehended, not forgotten. This has happened here before. And the end of it is always death.

I ask your understanding.

My brother asked for his inheritance and received the lot. Now everything he had is gone. Everything.
Because of him perhaps a young girl has laid down her clothes and gently drifted in and out of early spring. That bastard. Now they kill the fatted calf and offer him a ring. I was angry and would not go in.

Exposed my secret.

So here I stand. Uncelebrated servant of my father and his house. Worse than the beggars at his gate, scratching for bread.

Give me your secret dreams
and cherished sins.

Today my younger brother is exquisite. I mean
virtually luminescent. He basks in radiant father-
love.
There was a time when I knew what life was for.

May not be death.

A broken, secret longing to pour out this sense of
ought and overturn my father's symmetry.
A worthless younger brother did what I had only
thought.

Was it for me?

Still, have I transgressed? Or is it only he who must
be sacrificed, and turned, and then returned?

Exposed my secret.

And why this sense of wrath? My father, after all,
has killed the fatted calf and brought a robe and
shoes for one who squandered nothing but my
own most secret dreams and cherished sins.

I am so wooden. So alone. My
gestures freeze this side of touch.

I was angry and would not go in: therefore came
my father out.

I beg your intercessions.

Had my brother first repented, I would now be free. But anyone could see my father start to run while he was yet a long way off.

He will come running.

I wonder why my father did that?
So many things remain a mystery—not comprehended, not forgotten. This has happened here before. But the end of it may not be death.

What awesome love.

May not be death.

Just leaves me speechless.

Turned and then returned.

It was for me.

May not be death.

Sing alleluia.

It is not death.

THE LORD'S PRAYER

glo - ry   for _ ev - er and ev - er.   A – –   men. __

What Number Is This Moon?

SOLUMNAR was a sorcerer. He knew one important secret and six rather clever questions. Naturally, his power was awesome. "The mystery of life isn't a problem to solve," he said distinctly to the visitors assembled in his cave. "It's a reality to be experienced." On the wall behind him was an asymmetric disc that shined like gold. "Psychical wholeness transcends and integrates all natural occurrence. One's powers of meditation and hallucination must be developed to this end." A look of mild disinterest in his eyes, he turned from those present and created the illusion of becoming a tall column of flame. Out of the flame a stranger's voice cried, "Set them free. Set them free."

There was a protracted silence. Then Gwendolyn spoke. "It is but a mirage. The sorcerer desires to fill us with a sense of wonder."

"He has succeeded admirably," Roland said without taking his eyes from the column of flame. "I have never before been so disoriented."

By the very flatness of his voice, Gwendolyn could tell that Roland was already in a hypnoid state. In spite of her fear and an aching desire for rest, she called a challenge to the illusion Solumnar had created.

"We are not good. We are not innocent. We desire to go exploring, Solumnar. Tell me, if you can, what number is this moon?"

A brighter flame. The stranger speaking. "Your attention is given to irrelevant matters; you miss the mark. What you seek is certainly unobtainable."

Roland muttered, "No use, Gwendolyn. The whole thing is absurd."

"Solumnar," Gwendolyn repeated firmly, "we desire to go exploring."

Where a column of fire had been, the sorcerer stood calmly regarding his guests. "Please be patient," he said apparently without emotion. "We'll reach our destination soon enough. Nothing reveals itself apart from mind. Therefore, everything here is possible. The one reduction with which we must contend is that all of our instruments have been designed to tell time, not truth."

Roland again in monotone. "No final word. Dubious insight into primordial darkness. We shift our feet uneasily and call to the first stranger for provisional assurance. Thus, we fail to understand."

"Magnificent," Solumnar said, his long fingers now twisted together. "Just so! Fragments of freedom only. No final word here. But then, before you were born into this world, Roland, where were you?"

Gwendolyn began to realize that she no longer

wanted to be seeking. Weary of all questions, all answers, she dreamed of running from Solumnar's cave.

But a multiple hissing of voices confronted her. "Very unlikely," they said in unison.

"Solumnar," she managed the words with difficulty. "We are not good. We are not innocent. What number is this moon?"

"Mystery circle," Solumnar said, indicating the asymmetric, golden mandala on his wall. "No entrance. No exit. There are strange times for calling in accounts—even stranger times for their settlement. For instance, there is the matter of my own doubt which I am still unable to solve."

Roland twisted to the right and fixed a puzzled stare on Gwendolyn. "Where does the question you ask come from?"

"I need to see something which is stronger than death," she replied.

Solumnar's voice. "Truth is mixed with untruth. Salvation is a circle. Mystery circle. No entrance. No exit. Suffering and rejoicing, each of us struggles toward a sure and certain hope."

"You have not answered my question." Gwendolyn looked uneasy.

"My ignorance exceeds yours," replied Solumnar with a slight bow. "No use dreaming. If we can no longer cling to the mountain, then we must celebrate the fall."

Roland listened to the cave and the night outside. With an odd grimace he said, "Every word the sorcerer has spoken is true, Gwendolyn. Yet to embrace truth without simultaneously risking the self is only another form of death. Therefore, this moon is five. Number five moon."

"I had so hoped that it might be," Gwendolyn smiled. "Thank you, Roland. Thank you."

The mysterious column of flame reappeared and quickly stretched away into shadows. Soon, the cave and its occupants were gone. Only the asymmetric mandala remained. For a moment it seemed to hang in mid-air, shining like gold. Then the disc exploded into a liquid profusion of color. Jessica opened her violet eyes.

"Mystery circle," she said.

Wolf! Wolf!

Divide the sinners
            from the righteous, then?
The cost is high.
Existing men have
        found
        the price too
                    steep.
Precisely why
        we count ourselves
                    among
        the lost.
And cannot sleep.
All the years of
                    separation—
        measured pain.
Of self-abuse and
        lean, contemptuous
        striving to obtain
        what
        simply could not be:
A portion of contentment.
We judge and find
                    that

we ourselves
are judged—
Each time and place, concretely.
Rewards and
punishments
are quickly fudged.
Then lost in
space
completely.
For those who count
themselves among the
lost,
A note of exultation.
By grace,
to say that life
belongs to life
Erases all distinction.
Good news! The
scowling Tiger is
set free.
The cage
is standing open.
Cry Wolf! And make a
howling song with
· me.
Not even Death
can
stop
him.

Somewhat Faster

"I'm going to fast," he said.

"Have you tried to slow down?" I inquired kindly.

He looked at me deliberately. There was an attitude of charitable disbelief in his glance. "I'm going to *fast*," he repeated, pronouncing each word carefully, "not *too* fast."

"Oh." I managed a nervous smile. My nose itched.

He hadn't stopped staring at me.

"Listen, clucky, you know, *fast*, like in not eating."

"Holy cow!" I said with genuine admiration. "Boy, that's great. How long do you think you can keep it up?" His remark had brought me to the edge of my chair. I became highly animated.

"Forty days," was his matter-of-fact reply.

"You're putting me on."

"No, hell no."

A sense of awe came over me. My eyes filled with tears.

"You'll starve." He was going to commit suicide. I had never respected a man so much.

"Well," he blushed modestly, "it won't kill me, you know."

I didn't know. I wondered if I would have that kind of composure with death so near.

"Grapefruit juice," he whispered.

With alarm I realized it had begun already. He was hallucinating.

"Grapefruit juice," he said again. "That's what I'm giving up. It won't kill me to go forty days without grapefruit juice, for heaven's sake!"

My disappointment was keen—almost unbearable.

"What the hell's the matter with you, clucky?"

"Oh, nothing," I mumbled. My shoulders slumped. I sat back and shoved both hands into my pockets.

"How about you? Aren't you going to fast?"

"I suppose so," I nodded. "Yeah, you're right. I am going too fast."

HAIRCUT SONG

I don't like hair - cuts. I would rath - er play. And when-

ev - er I get a hair - cut, It ru - ins the rest of my

day. I wish I were a pan - da. I know what I'd do. I'd

nev - er get an-oth-er hair-cut, And I could live at the zoo.

Chorus

Mom-my, just you wait and see, I'll grow up and be a

pan - da. You won't e - ven know that it's me, and I'll

nev - er get a hair - cut a - gain.

HAIRCUT SONG

1. I don't like haircuts.
   I would rather play.
   And whenever I get a haircut,
   It ruins the rest of my day.

   I wish I were a panda.
   I know what I'd do.
   I'd never get another haircut,
   And I could live at the zoo.

   CHORUS:
   > *Mommy, just you wait and see;*
   > *I'll grow up and be a panda.*
   > *You won't even know that it's me,*
   > *And I'll never get a haircut again.*

2. I don't like vegetables.
   I'd rather eat a bug.
   One time when Mommy made me eat some,
   I threw up all over her rug.

   Vegetables and haircuts,
   Neither one is for me.
   But I never saw a panda eat a vegetable,
   So that's what I've decided to be.

CHORUS:

Mommy, just you wait and see;
I'll grow up and be a panda.
You won't even know that it's me,
And I'll never get a haircut again.

memory bag

1

spooky

lady never seems to
have time for
me
but i'll fix her
that's right got
a whole fine
traveling

case full of
odds
and ends from 8-1/2
on and one

memory

bag that's been
checked through
to

san francisco

2

hoo boy
stylistic overlay
and some
pretty raw emotion

keeps me

busier
than hell just
falling behind
in

my payments can't

help

the way i feel though
and like
the man says on
the fourth of july i

feel

good

3

been struggling like

this for

ever since i
can remember asking

what's

going on
which
is a fairly
long
time actually unless

you're counting on

it

and i was
so
that's
how come lukewarm

never

has been cool
anyway for

my money
and
i'm broke

4

haven't got
a
clue

regarding where the whole
mess
came from in
the first
place and neither have

you

by god yes
i suppose
we're in it together
or
something

like that

but no one ought to
be misled
into thinking communal
ignorance is half

as
comforting as it sounds

5

lost

myself recently
in the supermarket
somewhere between string
beans
and

puffed rice

should have turned
around
at the aisle marked
sundries i

guess but my

free expression has been
somewhat
inhibited ever since
they shot john

kennedy
and besides you

always run
the risk of ending up

in the bag

6

give me
the opportunity

and i'll meddle with
your life
too

not one shred of
pride remains
if it comes to
that
spent my last

four quarters

on the march
of dimes which left
me feeling sort of
down
and out when jerry
lewis made his nation
wide appeal

now there's commitment

for you whatever it takes
is what he gives

7

wish i was

a kangaroo
in a way but

only because they
get to
hop around and ride
in pouches
too

which is both free
and secure at the
same time bunch
of
baldfaced eyewash though
which copies

the style

of a congressional
hearing
since anyone can tell
you there's no

such thing as

free and secure at the same time

8

a memory bag

that's been
checked through to
san francisco
doesn't

cut much ice

in Minneapolis i'll
admit
but
it sure does
help keep
your

balance

if you end up
on
the slippery

slope

9

woke up yelling
again today

really doesn't pay
to eat large
amounts
of pizza before you

sleep

have a hard enough
time
distinguishing between
insight and
oversight anyway since
most
of the answers

raised

usually go unquestioned
and
no matter how
you
slice it

that's a problem

10

only thing worse
than a
dead faith is
a dead doubt
and

a faith

that boasts of certainty
would about
as
soon kill the spirit
as not

you bet

calls up all
my emotions of
last whenever it was
we were challenged
to
take the step from
faith

to fanaticism
i mean boy howdy that's
where
you know that
you know for

sure

11

spooky

lady never has
time for
me
but i'll fix
her

gonna dump the
whole insides
of my traveling
case on the

holy table

then wait
and
see what happens
ought to
be

quite a revelation

just as soon
dump my
memory bag too
only can't
since like i said

it's all chcckcd
through

to a station
in san

francisco

12

whiz bang

don't lose sight
of the
goal but better
not
claim the whole of

historical drama

represents
cosmic meddling
either
a jerry lewis style
commitment
to

god

and to life and
to redemption

would
do
just fine

whatever it takes
is
what you give
and especially
in these

intervening

years
it couldn't hurt
at all to
live

in a way that
keeps remembering
there's
no such thing as

free and secure

at
the same

time

NIGHT COMES EARLY, SUSAN

When I was jus a lit-tle boy, My moth-er __ called me close by her side And took my hand, __ but when I looked at her, ___ She be-gan to cry. I still re-call ___ that time; I was be-wil-dered and so I pulled my hand a-way and ran from the room. I could not un-der-stand __ And I would-n't stay. Night comes ear-ly, Sus-an. __ Bring your dolls, come in __ from play. I know that you won't un-der-

stand ____ But I'll take your hand ____ an - y - way. ____

CODA

Sus - an, good - night.　Turn out your light.　The

stars shine bright ____ For you. ____

NIGHT COMES EARLY, SUSAN

1. When I was just a little boy,
   My mother called me close by her side
   And took my hand, but when I looked at her,
   She began to cry.

   I still recall that time;
   I was bewildered and so I pulled
       my hand away
   And ran from the room. I could not understand
   And I wouldn't stay.

   CHORUS: *Night comes early, Susan.*
   Bring your dolls, come in from
       play.
   I know that you won't understand
   But I'll take your hand anyway.

2. The cold November wind has come
   And stolen all the years we had stored.
   I turned around and found an aging father
   A child no more.

   And could this be my little girl
   Who's standing with her dolls by the door?
   And is she really three? No, I'm mistaken,
   She's almost four.

[*chorus*]

Susan, goodnight.
Turn out your light.
The stars shine bright
For you. . . .

3. So when your dolls have all been put away,
And cold November winds have come,
Remember how I used to stand and wait
Til you got home.

Perhaps you'll understand just what it was
That I never said to you
And why I'd only hold you by the hand.
The words were few.

[*chorus*]

Night-Checkers

IMMANUEL KANT said there is something in the misfortune of our best friends that does not displease us. Linda said that wasn't true about her. And Tom said he didn't care. It was the beginning of a satisfactory relationship.

Of an evening Linda and Tom would sit on the front porch discussing progress in moral self-control. She was convinced that Kant was either unenlightened or dull. Tom said he had heard that old Immanuel was high on drugs most of the time and maybe this could explain how he got off on the wrong track. Linda thought why can't Tom ever be serious? More or less it was a time of courting and romance.

Before long Linda obtained a Bible from Pastor Marston and a theological education from Elaine Seeley. Night after night Tom thrilled to the threat of fiery annihilation that issued forth from her recounting of the Good News as she understood it.

St. John seemed to do the trick for Linda. I pray not for the world but for them which thou hast given me was her favorite part. She had never heard of realized eschatology, but she believed in moral self-control and so did Jesus, according to St. John.

Tom said he thought so, too. He said as far as he could see, the whole world was going to hell faster than anyone could imagine; only the good would survive. St. Paul used to smoke dope with Immanuel Kant, he added, and that's why it says in Romans: thou art inexcusable, O man, whosoever thou art that judgest—for wherein thou judgest another, thou condemnest thyself; for thou that judgest doest the same things. Linda countered with St. Matthew: Not everyone that saith unto me, Lord, Lord, shall enter into the Kingdom of heaven; but he that doeth the will of my Father which is in heaven. Then Tom kissed her on the mouth. They loved each other very much.

Tom was convinced that Linda simply didn't take sin seriously enough. She did not identify sin as an all-pervasive disease infecting the body of humanity. For Linda, it was an occasional malignancy that could be removed and thereafter eradicated. On this point Tom agreed with Professor Harrelson's metaphor. If God's perfection is an infinite distance from existing persons, then all are morally equidistant from God. It is by grace alone that the world is drawn unto and united with Him.

Tom was totally satisfied that St. Paul had long ago won the day as regards gospel proclamation, but he loved to listen while Linda told of the coming apocalypse. And, not incidentally, he loved Linda, too.

Justification by grace through faith was as alien

to Linda's thinking as it was to that of I St. John: whosoever is born of God doth not commit sin; for his seed remaineth in him: and he cannot sin, because he is born of God. Linda was not at all sure about Tom's progress in moral self-control. And sometimes she even wondered if he was born of God. Tom, for his part, was fond of repeating the Pauline formula: all have sinned and come short of the glory of God; being justified freely by his grace that is in Christ Jesus. The whole thing had the makings of a classic love affair.

When Linda's friend, Ellen Peterson, broke her leg in a skiing accident, even greater emotion came to the fore. Linda said thank God it wasn't *her* leg, and that got Tom started: Just like old Immanuel Kant used to chant when he was higher than a kite—there is something in the misfortune of our best friends that does not displease us. Linda pointed out that she wasn't pleased that Ellen Peterson had broken her leg; she was only pleased that she, Linda, had not. Almost the same, Tom said. Both manifestations of sin—separation of life from life. The two held each other tenderly and longed to be united.

The epistle of James says: Ye see then how that by works a man is justified, and not by faith only, Linda insisted as they walked hand in hand toward her house. Tom was tempted to agree, if for no other reason than that he felt their love was an admirable work, and he did, indeed, feel justified therein. Nevertheless, his Pauline bias got the best of him and he chose Romans 3:28 this time: therefore we conclude that a man is justified by faith without the deeds of the law.

Naturally, they were married and lived happily ever after.

But on the wedding night there was no mention of Immanuel Kant, St. John, St. James, or even St. Paul for that matter. Tom and Linda simply loved one another and offered their love to God.

I wonder if it would have surprised them to know that just outside in the darkness a large, silver wolf and a relatively small bird with fur were playing what appeared to be some form of nightcheckers. The bird hesitated, green eyes blinking. Patiently, the wolf said: It's your move, Arnold.

resurrection

darn right he did fella just like he said and left a lot
of people wondering if the whole thing might not
have been rigged by the special effects department

calculating type narrow eyes and all bet the whole
thing on number six black (good) took a pass on
number seven and hit the jackpot when it came
around to number one blue and gold and red and
orange

did time right along side of everyone else then
ended up in the lost and found department on his
way out but the authorities said he's got fever and
it's catching so anybody might get infected and
we'd better put a stop to that

awful hard to tell what is and what is not a hot
news item of course only this time no one asked to
see his credentials except for one missouri style
dude who no doubt simply couldn't keep his hands
off what had all the marks of a great story

well like gabriel heatter used to say there's good
news tonight and lots of confusion too i might add

since the implications of human morality are
hardly intimations of immortality only now it
looked like production might have called for a to-
tal re-write and gotten some pretty creative stuff
at that

definitely not a good social mixer he spent more
time messing up balancing acts than anything else
but i'll be damned if he didn't pay the price and
over the years more and more people have
claimed that this was the whole point of the origi-
nal tour and also the rationale behind his return
engagement

probably was too but even if it wasn't everybody's
gonna bet the whole stack on something or some-
body sooner or later and since history is downright
unrepeatable we don't get to witness the main
event but for the telling and the remembering
anyhow so how about you my friend or is that the
wrong question to be asking (yes)

great day in the morning who would have ever
thought the play would come around to me so
quickly planned to be much more cautious than
that and here i am in the tiger trap oh he was a
calculating type all right lost his life before he won
a blessed thing couldn't even bring himself to
speak his own mind which is what made him so
terrifying for the most part and the question i sur-
mise is how about me

hurry close the trap and set me free

FAITH, BROTHER

Chorus

Faith, Bro-ther, __ cour-age to - night. You are __ not a -
lone. _____ A - cross the whole wide world the
Spir - it is bright and we're final - ly com - ing home.
1. The Move - ment is strong, __ the peo - ple are wise. __
Steel in their arms, __ fire in their eyes. __ The
fu - ture be - longs __ to those who de - cide and
we're de - ci - ding now, so —

FAITH, BROTHER

CHORUS: *Faith, Brother, courage tonight.*
You are not alone.
Across the whole wide world
    the Spirit is bright
And we're finally coming home.

1. The Movement is strong,
       the people are wise.
   Steel in their arms,
       fire in their eyes.
   The future belongs to
       those who decide
   And we're deciding now, so

[*chorus*]

2. All our heroes gone,
       what a foolish plan—
   You don't kill an idea
       when you kill a man.
   I learned long ago
       all men soon will know
   When they killed Jesus it all started, so

[*chorus*]

3. I learned to hate and kill.
    I'll be damned if I will.
   That's one piece of learning
    I've forgotten.
   They're teaching you and me
    That by killing we'll be free.
   But we know that ain't so, so

[*chorus*]

4. Soon our lives are done,
    but the Movement will go on.
   We won't see the end of
    what we've started.
   But those who are to come
    Will take up what we've begun,
   And a new day will be dawning, so

[*chorus*]

Some Gospel Themes

FOR the love of Christ controls us, because we are convinced that one has died for all; therefore all have died. And he died for all, that those who live might live no longer for themselves but for him who for their sake died and was raised. From now on, therefore, we regard no one from a human point of view; even though we once regarded Christ from a human point of view, we regard him thus no longer. Therefore, if any one is in Christ, he is a new creation; the old has passed away, behold, the new has come. All this is from God, who through Christ reconciled us to himself and gave us the ministry of reconciliation; that is, God was in Christ reconciling the world to himself, not counting their trespasses against them, and entrusting to us the message of reconciliation. So we are ambassadors for Christ, God making his appeal through us. We beseech you on behalf of Christ, be reconciled to God. For our sake he made him to be sin who knew no sin, so that in him we might become the righteousness of God.

2 Corinthians 5:14–21

AΩ

And you he made alive, when you were dead through the trespasses and sins in which you once walked, following the course of this world, following the prince of the power of the air, the spirit that is now at work in the sons of disobedience. Among these we all once lived in the passions of our flesh, following the desires of body and mind, and so we were by nature children of wrath, like the rest of mankind. But God, who is rich in mercy, out of the great love with which he loved us, even when we were dead through our trespasses, made us alive together with Christ (by grace you have been saved), and raised us up with him, and made us sit with him in the heavenly places in Christ Jesus, that in the coming ages he might show the immeasurable riches of his grace in kindness toward us in Christ Jesus. For by grace you have been saved through faith; and this is not your own doing, it is the gift of God—not because of works, lest any man should boast. For we are his workmanship, created in Christ Jesus for good works, which God prepared beforehand, that we should walk in them.   *Ephesians 2:1–10*

AΩ

And Joseph took the body, and wrapped it in a clean linen shroud, and laid it in his own new tomb, which he had hewn in the rock; and he rolled a great stone to the door of the tomb, and departed. Mary Magdalene and the other Mary were there, sitting opposite the sepulchre.

Matthew 27:59–61

For there is no distinction; since all have sinned and fall short of the glory of God, they are justified by his grace as a gift, through the redemption which is in Christ Jesus, whom God put forward as an expiation by his blood, to be received by faith.

Romans 3:23–25

And he began to speak to them in parables. "A man planted a vineyard, and set a hedge around it, and dug a pit for the wine press, and built a tower, and let it out to tenants, and went into another country. When the time came, he sent a servant to the tenants, to get from them some of the fruit of the vineyard. And they took him and beat him and sent him away empty-handed. Again he sent to them another servant, and they wounded him in the head, and treated him shamefully. And he sent another, and him they killed; and so with many others, some they beat and some they killed. He had still one other, a beloved son; finally he sent him to them, saying, 'They will respect my son.' But those tenants said to one another, 'This is the heir; come, let us kill him, and the inheritance will be ours.' And they took him and killed him, and cast him out of the vineyard. What will the owner of the vineyard do? He will come and destroy the tenants and give the vineyard to others. Have you not read this scripture: 'The very stone which the builders rejected has become the head of the corner; this was the Lord's doing, and it is marvelous in our eyes'?" And they tried to arrest him, but feared the multitude, for they perceived that he had told the parable against them; so they left him and went away.   *Mark 12:1–12*

AΩ

And he said, "Go, and say to this people: 'Hear and hear, but do not understand; see and see, but do not perceive.' Make the heart of this people fat, and their ears heavy, and shut their eyes; lest they see with their eyes, and hear with their ears, and understand with their hearts, and and turn and be healed."   *Isaiah 6:9–10*

For God has consigned all men to disobedience, that he may have mercy upon all.   *Romans 11:32*

And he said to them, "Do not be amazed; you seek Jesus of Nazareth, who was crucified. He has risen, he is not here; see the place where they laid him. But go, tell his disciples and Peter that he is going before you to Galilee; there you will see him, as he told you." And they went out and fled from the tomb; for trembling and astonishment had come upon them; and they said nothing to anyone, for they were afraid.   *Mark 16:6–8*

Then as one man's trespass led to condemnation for all men, so one man's act of righteousness leads to acquittal and life for all men. For as by one man's disobedience many were made sinners, so by one man's obedience many will be made righteous. Law came in, to increase the trespass; but where sin increased, grace abounded all the more, so that, as sin reigned in death, grace also might reign through righteousness to eternal life through Jesus Christ our Lord.   *Romans 5:18–21*

AΩ

Therefore you have no excuse, O man, whoever you are, when you judge another; for in passing judgment upon him you condemn yourself, because you, the judge, are doing the very same things.   *Romans 2:1*

And he said, "There was a man who had two sons; and the younger of them said to his father, 'Father, give me the share of property that falls to me.' And he divided his living between them. Not many days later, the younger son gathered all he had and took his journey into a far country, and there he squandered his property in loose living. And when he had spent everything, a great famine arose in that country. And he began to be in want. So he went and joined himself to one of the citizens of that country, who sent him into his fields to feed swine. And he would gladly have fed on the pods that the swine ate; and no one gave him anything. But when he came to himself he said, 'How many of my father's hired servants have bread enough and to spare, but I perish here with hunger! I will arise and go to my father, and I will say to him. "Father I have sinned against heaven and before you; I am no longer worthy to be called your son; treat me as one of your hired servants."

And he arose and came to his father. But while he was yet at a distance, his father saw him and had compassion, and ran and embraced him and kissed him. And the son said to him, 'Father, I have sinned against heaven and before you; I am no longer worthy to be called your son.' But the father said to his servants, 'Bring quickly the best robe, and put it on him; and put a ring on his hand, and shoes on his feet; and bring the fatted calf and kill it, and let us eat and make merry; for this my son was dead and is alive again; he was lost and is found.' And they began to make merry.

"Now his elder son was in the field; and as he came and drew near to the house, he heard music and dancing. And he called one of the servants and asked what this meant. And he said to him, 'Your brother has come, and your father has killed the fatted calf, because he has received him safe and sound.' But he was angry and refused to go in. His father came out and entreated him, but he answered his father, 'Lo, these many years I have served you, and I never disobeyed your command; yet you never gave me a kid, that I might make merry with my friends. But when this son of yours came, who has devoured your living with harlots, you killed for him the fatted calf!' And he said to him, 'Son, you are always with me, and all that is mine is yours. It was fitting to make merry and be glad, for this your brother was dead, and is alive; he was lost, and is found.' "   *Luke 15:11–32*

AΩ

Always and for everything giving thanks in the name of our Lord Jesus Christ to God the Father.
Ephesians 5:20

I am praying for them; I am not praying for the world but for those whom thou hast given me, for they are thine; all mine are thine, and thine are mine, and I am glorified in them.   *John 17:9–10*

Not every one who says to me, 'Lord, Lord,' shall enter the kingdom of heaven, but he who does the will of my Father who is in heaven.
Matthew 7:21

For we hold that a man is justified by faith apart from works of law.   *Romans 3:28*

You see that a man is justified by works and not by faith alone.   *James 2:24*

The stone which the builders rejected
  has become the chief cornerstone.
This is the Lord's doing;
  it is marvelous in our eyes.
                  Psalm 118:22–23

ΑΩ

But if it is by grace, it is no longer on the basis of works; otherwise grace would no longer be grace.   *Romans 11:6*

No one born of God commits sin; for God's nature abides in him, and he cannot sin because he is born of God. By this it may be seen who are the children of God, and who are the children of the devil: whoever does not do right is not of God, nor he who does not love his brother.   *1 John 3:9–10*

But whatever gain I had, I counted as loss for the sake of Christ. Indeed I count everything as loss because of the surpassing worth of knowing Christ Jesus my Lord. For his sake I have suffered the loss of all things, and count them as refuse, in order that I may gain Christ and be found in him, not having a righteousness of my own, based on law, but that which is through faith in Christ, the righteousness from God that depends on faith; that I may know him and the power of his resurrection, and may share his sufferings, becoming like him in his death, that if possible I may attain the resurrection from the dead. Not that I have already obtained this or am already perfect; but I press on to make it my own, because Christ Jesus has made me his own. *Philippians 3:7–12*

ΑΩ

For I am sure that neither death, nor life, nor angels, nor principalities, nor things present, nor things to come, nor powers, nor height, nor depth, nor anything else in all creation, will be able to separate us from the love of God in Christ Jesus our Lord. *Romans 8:38–39*